If it happens to your child, it happens to you!

CHRISTINE A. GOLDER

**IF IT HAPPENS TO YOUR CHILD,
IT HAPPENS TO YOU!**
Copyright © 2021 by Christine A. Golder, M.S.W.
Originally Published in 1987 by R&E Publishers, California

All rights reserved. No part of this publication may be reproduced, distributed, or transmitted in any form or by any means, including photocopying, recording, or other electronic or mechanical methods, without the prior written permission of the publisher or author, except in the case of brief quotations embodied in critical reviews and certain other noncommercial uses permitted by copyright law.

Although every precaution has been taken to verify the accuracy of the information contained herein, the author and publisher assume no responsibility for any errors or omissions. No liability is assumed for damages that may result from the use of information contained within.

Library of Congress Control Number: 2021908441
ISBN-13:   Paperback: 978-1-64749-449-0
           Epub: 978-1-64749-450-6

Printed in the United States of America

GoToPublish LLC
1-888-337-1724
www.gotopublish.com
info@gotopublish.com

CONTENTS

Introduction vii
1. Child Sexual Assault —
   An Overview of the problem 1
2. From Assault to Disclosure 9
3. Report and the Legal System: What to Expect ... 23
4. Parental Dilemmas 31
5. What Else Can Be Done 43
References 47
Appendix A 51
About the Author 53

I dedicate this book to the memory of
Roslyn Reichler

INTRODUCTION

I chose to write this book on how sexual abuse impacts on the entire family. My concept is that the parents are as victimized by this crisis as is the child, although they are affected in different ways. The entire family system is thrown into a state of crisis or disequilibrium as they try to cope with the horror that their child was a victim of a sexual crime by an adult outside the family.[1] The perpetrator could be a neighbor, friend, baby-sitter, school personnel, or, in rarer instances, a stranger. Sexual abuse, molestation and rape is to be distinguished from incest, which involves a relative or family member. The effects of incest have even more profound pathological implications from within the family structure that must be addressed. This is a different problem which will not be a focus of this book.

In researching available literature, I found most of the information on the topic of sexual molestation of children addressed preventative issues. The preponderance of literature on treatment issues focused on incest, which historically has been a topic of more in-depth research.

---

1 By family, I will use the definition of all members of the child's household or people that live with the child.

Child sexual abuse outside the family has been an area that in the early 1980's gained national visibility since the uncovering of institutional abuse at day-care centers in California and in the Bronx, New York.

Exploiting children through pornography is a form of child abuse in which children are portrayed as sexual objects. Although research has not yet been able to correlate pornographic exploitation of women and children to increased incidence of rape and sexual crime, it is a form of social casting into the role of victim or sexual object. This is another vast related area that will not be covered in this book.

There are several different aspects of the problem. I intend to review what may occur from the time of the child's disclosure to the termination of therapy. My main focus will be on the family's role and reactions and its significance.

My interest developed while working with parent groups of sexually abused children. One agency in which I work specifically serves the needs of victims of domestic violence, rape, sexual assault and incest. Over the course of two years, I have co-led groups of parents whose children were victims of sexual assault. The parents are able to use the group to share similar concerns, feelings and frustrations regarding the ordeal their child had experienced and how it impacted on the entire family. Some expressed the need for a "how to" book that would better prepare them for what to expect and how to cope with the situation. Another complaint was the scarcity of books in the library that dealt specifically with child sexual assault. They felt there was nothing addressed to parents to help their children and themselves after the assault has occurred.

Preventative programs called "street-proofing your child" have been introduced in the schools and pre-schools. Also, there are now children's books and TV programs that teach children about what is appropriate touch. But, again, there is still a lack of information addressing the problem in the aftermath of the occurrence. It is this paucity and my awareness of the existent need for such information that prompted me to write such a handbook. I hope that it will serve to help those parents of child victims that feel isolated, helpless and victimized themselves, due to an unspeakable crime and society's choice to largely ignore it.

My references to observations taken from the parent groups will be generalized and will exclude any identifying information regarding the participants. The first chapter will present an overview of the problem and a review of the literature on the topic. The second chapter focuses on the victim and how the abuse will affect both children and adolescents. The nature of the abuse will also be described in detail. Parents often have questions about what sort of person could do such a hideous thing. Part of this chapter addresses the perpetrator as well. Chapter Three gives a step- by-step approach of what to expect in encountering the legal system and the many difficulties that can arise. Parents need to be prepared for how the slow-moving proceedings can impact themselves and their child. Chapter Four deals entirely with the parent's feelings and reactions. This chapter offers parents ways to cope with their child's feelings in relation to their own. The final chapter offers creative suggestions for parents who want to do something more about the problem.

1. CHILD SEXUAL ASSAULT – AN OVERVIEW OF THE PROBLEM

Child sexual assault is three times as common as child battering and is still considered grossly under-reported.[1] The term sexual abuse in reference to children means the "exposure of the child to sexual stimulation that is inappropriate for the child's age, level of psycho-sexual development and role in the family."[2]

This problem knows no economic or social boundaries.[3] In 1981 the National Study of Child Neglect and Abuse Reporting found sexual maltreatment has shown the greatest increase in reported cases relative to all types of abuse and neglect of children.[4] Approximately 33 percent of all sexual abuse cases known to police involve children.[5] Statistics give evidence that one in five girls and one in eleven boys are sexually abused before the age of eighteen.[6] These statistics are based on reported cases however. Of a sampling

---

1   p. 47, "Suviving Sexual Assault", Congdon and Weed Inc., New York. 1982
2   p.11, An Annotated Bibliography of Child Sexual Abuse, Benjamin Schleslinger.
3   p. 35, Sexual Assault: Confronting Rape in America, Gager & Schurr: Grosset & Dunlap, New York. 1976.
4   p. 369, "Sexual Abuse of Young Children", Khan & Sexton; Clinical Pediatrics, Vol. 22, No. 5.
5   Ibid.
6   6p. 557, "The Justice System and the Sexual Abuse of Children", Jon R. Conte, Social Service Review, University of Chicago, Dec. 1984.

of adult women, 35 percent of the respondents stated that they had been victims of sexual abuse involving bodily contact before the age of eighteen.[7] This astonishing statistic hints that we are only realizing a "tip of the iceberg" compared to the true probability of the problem's vastness. Another strong implication points to the need for national prevention programs which fortunately are being implemented in school systems throughout the country. We cannot overlook another ugly fact regarding this crime. Preschoolers and infants as young as four months have been victims of rape and sexual assault.[8] Therefore, we must also develop programs of community education to reach parents of very young children with information regarding prevention of sexual abuse.

Even in the sexually open society in which we live today, child molestation is still not a subject that people feel comfortable discussing. This very silence on the topic or reaction of disbelief contributes to the perpetuation of the problem. In denying such a thing could happen to the happy. well-adjusted child, we may overlook the first signs that signal to us that there is a problem our child is experiencing but might find difficult to talk about. (An in-depth examination of symptomatic behavior will be discussed in a later chapter.)

Parents and teachers have conveyed to children that they have to obey, to be quiet, to be good and listen to adults. These broad and indiscriminate messages create the perfect victim.[9] Sexuality is rarely discussed openly with children

---

7 Ibid.
8 p. 3, Khan & Sexton.
9 p. 4, "The Sexually Abused Boy", Preventing Sexual Abuse, Vol. 1, No. I Spring 1986, Alexander Saphiris.

so they receive the implicit message that there is something mysterious and secretive about it. Girls especially are socialized to feel shame and guilt about their sexuality. Having been trained to passivity and silence, they grow up accepting all forms of subordination to boys and men around them: excellent training for victimization. Boys are socialized to fear being called a "sissy or gay" and will maintain silence against the threat of their masculinity being questioned. Accepting a gift or not resisting and being able to prevent the abuse creates feelings of guilt and shame which incorporate a sense of shared responsibility for the occurrence. This is a "blame the victim" attitude which permeates our society's mode of thinking, especially in cases of adolescent rape. The myth of the seductive child stems back to the roots of psychoanalytic theory. Freud, himself, did not believe his female patients who described their experience of sexual assault. He attributed their "fantasies" to a theory he later developed and named the Oedipus Complex.[10]

Child sexual abuse is certainly not a new problem given rise due to our sexually permissive modern society. Florence Rush researched as far back as Greek and Roman civilizations to document sexual practices involving children. She gives an extensive historical perspective that leads up through the ages to our modern times, giving evidence that children have always existed as sexual objects for adult amusement and pleasure.[11] - As noted above, some adult-child sex practices such as rites of passage and child marriages were

---

10   p. 60, Gager & Schurr
11   p. 95, The Best Kept Secret, Florence Rush, Mc-Craw-1 fill, 1980.

sanctioned by different societies and accepted as normative behavior.

So why does child sexual abuse still exist today? No one can ignore the fact that 95 percent of the perpetrators of girls and 80 percent of the perpetrators of boys are men.[12] How are men socialized differently which makes them more prone to victimizing children? Let us examine these differences as described by David Finkelhor.

    a. Women learn earlier and more completely to distinguish sexual and non-sexual forms of affection, so when men are feeling dependent and need affection, they are more likely to look for fulfillment in a sexual form even with an inappropriate partner. Women can get needs met also with children without prevailing upon the relationships.[13]

    b. Men grow up viewing heterosexual success as much more important to their gender identities. When their egos suffer an insult, they are more likely to feel a need for sex to reconfirm their adequacy, even if a child is the only available partner. Sex with children may be a weak confirmation, but it is still some confirmation.[14]

    c. Men are socialized to be able to focus their sexual interest around sex acts isolated from the context of

---

12   30-79, Ibid.
13   p. 12, Child Sexual Abuse, David Finkelhor; The Free Press, 1984.
14   Ibid.

a relationship. This is illustrated in their greater interest in pornography. Women, in contrast, are taught to focus on whole, romantic relationships. Men can experience arousal because the partner, even though a child, had the "right" kind of genitals or could engage in the desired sex act. [15]

d. Men are socialized to see persons younger and smaller than themselves as appropriate sexual partners, whereas women view appropriate partners as persons older and larger.[16]

e. Another aspect of male socialization not mentioned by Finkelhor, is the equation of masculinity with aggression and a form of supremacy or predator role that implies a victim.

As adult women become more assertive and stand up for their rights, children remain as the perfect powerless victims, without a voice. Despite protests of many feminist groups, the media continues to promote the sexualization of children and teens in sensual magazine ads, billboards and TV commercials. Child pornography is big business.

In order for sexual abuse to be eliminated, men need to be allowed to practice affection and dependency in relationships that do not involve sex, such as male-to-male friendships and nurturant interaction with children so that they do not remain removed from them. If they can experience them as young person instead of objects, they will be less

---
15 p. 12, 13. Ibid.
16 p. 13, Ibid.

likely to exploit their bodies. The accomplishment of sex must be de-emphasized as a criterion of male adequacy. For men to enjoy sexual relationships based on equality, they must learn to be more comfortable relating to women at the same level of maturity and competence.

To keep men away from children is not a solution to the problem of child sexual abuse. Instead, if men were allowed to take more responsibility for the care of children from infancy forward, they may become better able to identify with children's well-being and learn to enjoy deeply affectionate relationships that have no sexual component.[17] Of course, not all men become child abusers. There are certain individual psychological and experiential factors that predispose a person for child molestation. These include arrested emotional development, a need to feel powerful and controlling, reenactment of childhood trauma to undo the hurt; narcissistic identification with self as a young child; childhood sexual experience that was traumatic or strong conditioning and modeling of sexual interest in children by someone else.[18]

There are also factors that predispose the perpetrator's ability to overcome a child's resistance: If the child is emotionally insecure or deprived, if the child lacks the knowledge of sexual abuse, if the child trusts the offender, or if the offender attempts to coerce the child who is virtually defenseless against an adult.[19]

So often we tell our children to be wary of strangers, but in 75 to 80 percent of reported cases

---
17   Ibid.
18   Ibid.
19   p. 56, Ibid.

of child sexual assault, the offender was known to the victims and family.[20] Of reported assaults. 60 percent occur in the victim or assailant's home.[21] Children need to be armed with knowledge about their bodies, what is appropriate touch and that they have the right to say "no" and tell someone. These are preventative issues that every child must learn in order to be better prepared to face the possibility of sexual assault. Recently. several television shows have been aired that bring out the salient issues of child sexual abuse, but more education is needed, especially for preschoolers, incorporated into their cartoon and children shows. If there is no personal safety program being taught in the school district, this should certainly be a prioritized concern for the local P.T.A. to address.

Appendix A consists of prevention materials to be utilized as a resource for parents. The remainder of this book will deal with issues surrounding the problem in relation to its actual occurrence.

---

20   p. 57, Ibid.
21   p. 47, "Surviving Sexual Assault".

2. FROM ASSAULT TO DISCLOSURE

The ability to lure a child into a sexual relationship is based upon the all-powerful and dominant position of the adult or older adolescent perpetrator which is in sharp contrast to the child's age, size, dependency and subordinate position. This authority and power enables the perpetrator, implicitly or directly to coerce the child into sexual compliance.[1]

Sexuality between an adult and child may range from exhibitionism to intercourse, but can include a wide range of behaviors:

a. Exposing children to adult nudity or disrobing in front of children.
b. Adult genital exposure and directing the child's attention to observe them.
c. Observation of the child undressing, bathing, excreting or urinating.
d. Prolonged or French kissing or caressing.
e. Fondling the child's body or requesting this of the child to perform on the adult's body.

---

1   p. 9, Handbook of Clinical Intervention in Child Sexual Abuse, Suzanne M. SGroi; C.C. Heath & Co.

f. Masturbation, either observed or participatory.
g. Oral-genital contact.
h. Digital penetration of the anus or vaginal opening or use of inanimate objects for this purpose.
i. Dry humping, often resulting in ejaculation onto child's body without penetration.
j. Penile penetration of vagina or anus.[2]

Most sexual assaults of children follow a pattern of gradually escalating activities. It may begin as tickling beyond the point of a game or touching on the breasts or buttocks, but acting as if it is accidental. The child may be aware only of a sense of discomfort. This gradual escalation of contact leaves room for alert children to get help if they have enough information to know what they are experiencing is not alright.[3]

Contrary to the fear that small children will be forced to have sexual intercourse, the most common forms of sexual assault are fondling and exhibitionism.[4]

The Perpetrators

Lynn Daugherty distinguishes between the molester and rapist as having different motivations.[5] Child molesters abuse children to meet their emotional and sexual needs. They are attracted to

---

[2] p. 11-12, Ibid.
[3] p. 11, No More Secrets, Caren Adams & Jennifer Fay Jennifer Fay, Network Publications, Santa Cruz, 1984.
[4] Ibid. 28Ihid.
[5] p.22, "Why Me?" Lynn B. Daugherty, Mother Cour-29p. 24, Ibid. age Press; 1984, Racine, Wisconsin. 30ibid.

children as sex objects and are seeking acceptance or companionship. Rapists use and abuse children through sexual acts mainly to satisfy other needs and desires. which include power, anger and sadistic feelings. Both have serious psychological problems. Their other commonality is that their relationships with other adults, especially sexual relationships, are very different. The child molester avoids the threat by turning to children as a safer substitute. The rapist denies his fears by striking out and attacking children. Another type of individual that could abuse children is the sociopath. This person is extremely self-centered and cares little for the welfare of others. His impulsive desires for excitement are more important and may sexually abuse a child "for kicks".[6]

Molesters and rapists can be broken down into several categories. Fixated child molesters or pedophiles are "stuck" at a child-like or adolescent level of psychological development. They have never developed the ability to relate comfortably to adults their own age, especially adult women. They find children more sexually exciting than adults. Their sexual interest in children often becomes compulsive and they cannot stop even if they want to or try to. Sexual contacts usually are carefully planned.[7]

The regressed molester has developed some social skills that allow them to interact with other adults, especially women. They often marry and have families. But under a great deal of stress, they "regress" to relationships with children. Although their primary sexual orientation is toward people of

---

6   p. 27, Ibid. 311bid.
7   p. 23, Ibid. 32p. 218, "Sexual Abuse of Adolescents". Jerome

their own age, they have poor resources for handling stress. They replace their difficult relationships with other adults with involvement with children and meet their emotional needs through sexual activity.[8] Regressed child molesters usually choose girls as their victims and imagine that she is really much older. In the mind of the perpetrator, he/she thinks of her as an adult, therefore, she becomes an appropriate sexual partner.[9]

Most sexual assaults of children involve repeated incidences of non-violent molestation, but sometimes children are forcibly raped. There are several different motives for rape. The anger rapist is often physically brutal. He is taking out his rage at other people or frustrating situations on his victims. His interest is to hurt and degrade his victim. The anger rapist often acts without planning and then escapes.[10] The power rapist feels inadequate and insecure. His goal is the sexual conquest and control of the victim which makes him feel powerful. He uses only enough force as is necessary to "win" his victim. He needs to believe that the victim wanted to have sex with him, and even enjoyed it. This way he can feel like a desirable, powerful person.[11] The sadistic rapist is rare. For these severely disturbed individuals, sexuality and aggression become mixed. They get sexual enjoyment and satisfaction from tormenting and injuring victims. Such rapes often end in murder.[12] In gang rapes, each may have his own motive. One may be venting his anger on the victim.

---

8   p. 24, Ibid.
9   p. 25, Ibid.
10   Ibid.
11   p. 26, Ibid.
12   Ibid.

Another may be trying to prove his power to the other rapists or to the victim. Still another may be trying to gain acceptance from his buddies.[13]

The Child Victim

Sexual abuse does have an emotional impact on the child. Victims who do not receive any services may have longstanding problems. The degree of impact is affected by several variables. Quick and responsible intervention goes a long way to alleviate the impact.[14]

The first variable is the relationship between the offender and the victim. We must assess the depth of the relationship between the offender and the victim.[15] We must also assess the depth of the relationship according to the child's definition. A crime committed by a total stranger is less likely to be as traumatic as sexual abuse by a trusted and loved parent. The offender may be a stranger to the parents, but the child may have established a relationship with the offender which in the child's mind was based on trust and love. The second variable is the duration of sexual abuse. Rather than make the mistake of treating a one-time incident with the horror of a mass murder, we must de-escalate our reaction appropriately to involved concern. It may have been an unpleasant experience the child would not want to go through again, but children that have had to live with regular abuse are more impacted as their survival becomes more connected with it.[16] Another variable affecting

---

[13] p. 27, Ibid.
[14] p. 139, The Silent Children, Linda Tschirhart San-ford, 1980; New York: Anchor Press/Doubleday.
[15] Ibid.
[16] p. 140, Ibid.

the child victim is the type of sexual abuse involved in the molestation. Victims of penetration, sodomy and violence will be visibly impacted by the injury. Other forms of sex play, such as exhibitionism and mutual masturbation may be perceived by the younger child as a "game". We cannot impose our adult interpretations of the sex act on the child and make assumptions about any given form of sexual abuse and how it will affect the individual child.[17]

In all cases, a sensitive and thorough physical examination should take place so the doctor can reassure the victim that his or her body has not changed or been damaged because of the abuse. Especially in cases of a combination of physical and sexual abuse, the victim can benefit front long-range intervention to deal with feelings of helplessness and anger resulting from the offense.[18]

The child's age and developmental level must also be taken into account. Parents are sometimes amazed at the calmness of their young child who has been molested by the baby-sitter or neighbor. When the police arrive, the child may be more fascinated with the squad car and the uniforms than concerned with discussing what happened. An older child that knows what has happened is wrong, may feel violated as well as responsible for the crime. We should not demand trauma from a child too young to display the disdain we think he/she should feel.[19]

The most important variable is the reaction of the parents or other important people around the victim. Knowing that the significant adults in

---

17 Ibid.
18 p. 141, Ibid.
19 Ibid.

the youngster's life believe and do not blame the victim for what happened is the single and most important factor in preventing the abuse from becoming a life-destroying event. Some parents will insist on a confrontation with the offender, which can be just as traumatic for the victim as the sexual exploitation. Victims need to be reassured by parents or parent figures that they will be taken care of and protected. Many children fear that they will be rejected or abandoned by their families because of the abuse. They decide not to make trouble and keep the secret. They also fear the offender's retaliation, which may be an expressed threat. The child also needs to be reassured that she or he is still loved and is not a bad person because this has happened. They want to know that their safety will be insured, but a vigilante movement can have a traumatic backlash on a child, believing she/he will be responsible for the terrible things that happen to the offender. There may have been positive aspects for the child in the relationship with the offender that increases the child's feelings of guilt and responsibility for what happened. If the child has been warned not to be with a certain person or in a certain place where the abuse occurred, he/she may interpret the molestation as punishment for disobeying and be more fearful of disclosure to the parent for this reason. The parents should convey to the child that although they are not happy about the disobedience, the child did not deserve this to happen to him/her; the offender was very wrong and the disobedience is forgiven.[20]

There are behavioral changes that may manifest during and/or after the molestation. Symptoms

---
20   p. 143-4, Ibid.

can also change from what they were before the silence was broken and after the discovery of the offense. Some of these are:

1. Loss of appetite
2. Nightmares
3. Fear of a specific person
4. Running away
5. Changes in sleep patterns
6. Unprovoked crying spells
7. Bed wetting
8. Refusal to go to school
9. Fear of strange people or places
10. Fear of playing or sitting alone
11. Suicidal or emotional withdrawal
12. Clinging to a significant adult
13. Changes in fantasy life
14. Taking excessive baths[21]

Other behavioral indications include:

1. Overly compliant behavior
2. Inappropriate sex play with peers or toys
3. Pseudo-mature behavior or detailed, age-inappropriate understanding of sexual behavior
4. Poor peer relations or inability to make friends
5. Lack of trust towards adults
6. Inability to concentrate in school
7. Sudden drop in school performance
8. Extraordinary fears of males
9. Seductive behavior with males

---

[21] pp. 147-8, Ibid.

10. Regressive behavior
11. Depression
12. Suicidal feelings[22]

Any significant change in a child's pattern of behavior can indicate any number of problems a child may be having which may not necessarily be related to sexual abuse. These changes should raise concern and signal to a parent something may be wrong and warrant looking into. Active listening is an important skill for the parent or significant adult to utilize in the youngster's disclosure process. Children often find it very difficult to tell their parents what happened because they fear a powerful emotional reaction that they will not be able to handle. This is why they may choose to tell another adult outside the family that they trust, or a peer that they hope will help keep their secret.

The Adolescent Victim

If the abuse has occurred over a number of years, often disclosure does not occur until adolescence. Extensive review of rape research notes that adolescents constitute the largest group of sexual assault victims reported to the police.[23]

Statistics also indicate that those who are at highest risk for rape are young women, ages 13-25, with low socio-economic status.[24] Rape trauma syndrome is described as physical, emotional and behavioral stress reactions that result from the person being forced with a life-threatening event

---
[22] pp. 40-41, Sgroi.
[23] p. 3, Sexual Assault Among Adolescents, Suzanne S. Ageton, D.C. Heath & Co., 1983, Lexington, Massachu-setts.
[24] p. 395, A Literature Review on Sexual Abuse Literature, Journal of Nurse-Midwifery, Vol. 29, No. 6, Nov.?, Dec. '84.

that results in acute disorganization and long-term reorganization of one's life. Physical complaints may surface in the form of soreness all over the body or in the specific areas attacked. Sleeping and eating disturbances are common. Emotionally, victims begin to have fears of physical injury, mutilation and death. They may also feel humiliation, degradation, guilt, shame, embarrassment, self-blame, anger and revenge. They try to block out the thought of the rape, but cannot. They try to mentally undo or redo the situation. The long-time process of reorganization includes changes in lifestyles, nightmares and phobias. Some victims find difficulty carrying out normal routines. A preoccupation with details of the assault or an assailant is also reported. A global fear of people, fear of sex (especially if the rape was the first sexual experience), fear of being alone or in crowds and fear of men are also long-reaching effects the trauma has on individuals. If they receive help, 80 to 90 percent of victims will return to normal functioning.[25]

Initially, reactions to sexual assault arouse a wide range of conflicting feelings in victims. Below are some common responses to these reactions:

Emotional shock and numbness: Why am I so calm?

Why can't I cry?

Disbelief: Did it really happen? Why me?

Embarrassment: What will people think?I can't tell my family.

Shame: I feel dirty. Is there something wrong with me now?

---

25 p. 396, Ibid.

Guilt: Did I do something to make that happen to me? If only I had...

Depression: How am I going to go on? I feel so tired and hopeless.

Powerlessness: Will I ever be in control again?

Disorientation: I'm having trouble getting through the day; everything is so overwhelming.

Re-triggering: I keep having flashbacks. I wish I could make them stop.

Denial: Wasn't it just a fake? I'm okay!

Fear: Will I ever get over this? I'm afraid I'm going crazy. Am I safe? The nightmares.

Anxiety: I'm a nervous wreck. 1 have trouble breathing..

Anger: I want to kill him.[26]

It is not uncommon for rape victims to wonder whether or not they will ever feel "normal" again. "Teenage girls may not always identify themselves as victims of force in peer-rape, otherwise known as acquaintance- or date-rape. They confuse their own submission with consent. They can be taken advantage of and trapped because of:

1. the fear of getting in trouble.
2. their inexperience and lack of information about sexuality
3. their own need to enter the world of love and romance.
4. the numbers of new people in their lives.
5. their trust of others and the willingness to think they have misunderstood another's intentions.

---

[26] pp. 26_7, Surviving Sexual Assault, Rochel Gross-man, Congdon & Weed, Inc., New York. 1982.

6. their belief that if they are good, good things will happen and if bad things happen, they must have deserved it.[27]

Teens need to realize that it's still rape "even if they know the guy". Most often teenagers are likely to encounter peer-rape in situations of sexual bargaining rather than interactions that seem violent. Verbal pressure may be followed by grabbing or shoving.[28]

Popular coercions are: "If you love me, you will", or "Everybody's doing it". The line between seduction and rape is rarely drawn.

Some of the reasons adolescents don't tell their parents about an assault is because they are afraid of upsetting them. They may feel a certain loyalty to the offender, they blame themselves, or think they broke some rule when the assault occurred.[29] Most often they tell their friends. When the parents do learn of the assault, they can be most helpful if they tell their youngster the following:

1. "I believe you".
2. "I'm glad you told me".
3. "It's not your fault".
4. "I'll do my best to protect you".[30]

What else is necessary and helpful is to see that the youngster receives basic medical care while respecting the need for privacy. Assist in deciding about police reporting and legal proceedings, but

---

27 p. 4, Nobody Told Me it Was Rape, Caren Adams & Jennifer Fay, Network Publications, Santa Cruz, 1984
28 Ibid
29 p. 24, Ibid
30 Ibid

let the youngster be in control of the final decision. Confirm the youngster's perception of the assault. Provide reassurance about the youngster's ability to talk of him/herself while allowing comfort and safety. A parent's concerns are different from that of the adolescent.[31]

The adolescent should not be overburdened with the parents' fears. The youngster needs help to seek professional counseling through a rape crisis center, but they cannot be forced to attend. It is important for the parents to reassure them that they are loved and that the parents are supportive of them in this crisis, but the parents cannot take over for them or make decisions for them. The youngster must feel that they do still have control over their lives so as to reduce the overwhelming powerlessness that stems from the assault.

The feelings of helplessness, powerlessness and loss of safety and control have a major impact on the immediate and ultimate recovery from the rape trauma. Legal prosecution often prolongs the trauma. The victim experiences a loss of self-esteem. He/she may feel fragmented; that he/she may never be a whole person again.[32] Crisis intervention is essential for recovery through the acute phase of the syndrome.

---

31 Ibid
32 p. 218, "Sexual Abuse of Adolescents". Jerome Shem, Adolescent Sexuality; Vol. 71, No. 6, June '82.

3. REPORT AND THE LEGAL SYSTEM: WHAT TO EXPECT

Few parents and children are prepared or knowledgeable about what to do after finding out about their child's sexual assault. Most communities have a rape crisis hotline or agency that they can call for information and assistance through the difficult ordeal of reporting the crime and encountering the legal system. They may request that an advocate be present to accompany them and their child throughout this process to offer support and provide explanations regarding each step in the procedures to follow.

Sometimes the child and family may not be ready to make a report right away and may wish to seek counseling first about the trauma. Even if the decision to delay pressing charges is made, a medical examination should be performed as soon as possible. It is up to the hospital and doctor to make a report if physical trauma is evidenced. Emergency rooms are best equipped to treat victims of assault or rape by collecting specimens and testing for venereal disease and pregnancy. If the family decides to utilize a private physician, be sure the examiner knows what is required and is willing to participate and even appear in court as a witness, if necessary. The medical examination should include:

1. A good overall history.
2. Identification of all trauma with emphasis on genital, rectal and oral trauma.
3. Careful description of genital anatomy, even if without trauma, such as size of vaginal opening, condition of hymen ring, etc.
4. Tests for presence of sperm in vagina or elsewhere on body, blood test for syphilis and cultures for gonorrhea from throat, urethra, urine, vagina, and rectum.
5. Documentation of genito-urinary or rectal foreign objects.
6. Pregnancy tests for adolescent girls.[33]

Medical procedures are frightening and upsetting experiences for children, especially if they have been sexually assaulted. The medical examiners should be asked to explain to the parent and the child what is going to happen and why. Someone should make sure the child understands in his or her own language. The child should be allowed to ask questions. The parent should be allowed to remain in the examining room. Some hospitals have policies against the parent being present. The child may require a local anesthesia in order for the pelvic or rectal exam to be performed, especially if there is trauma. It is crucial for the child to know

---

[33] p. 154, Sexual Assault of Children and Adolescents, Burges, Groth, Holmstrom & Sgroi, D.C. Health & Co., Lexington, Massachusetts, 1978.

that he/she can stop the examination at any point that it becomes painful or frightening. Refusing to allow the child this control can be experienced as an additional assault. The child must be prepared that the examination may hurt and it is okay to cry if they need to. The child needs to be reassured and to feel safe and in control. Children need to know that their bodies are still okay and have not been changed as a result of the assault.[34]

Parents must keep in mind that most cases of sexual abuse of children lack laboratory or physical evidence of sexual contact. When venereal disease does appear in a child, it should be considered an indication of sexual abuse unless proven otherwise.[35]

Insensitive handling of child sexual abuse cases by the justice system personnel can lead to system-induced trauma; such as an attitude of disbelief communicated to the victim and thereby invalidating the experience; multiple interviews with various members of the justice system involving the child having to recount the details of the experience and relive it; disruptions in the child's life resulting from the many hearing dates and court appearances required.[36] Many communities have responded to the special needs of children and the realizations that interviewers have to have an understanding of the dynamics of sexual abuse in order to deal with child victims effectively. Such special Sex Crime Task Forces may exist in some areas. They possibly can recommend a sensitive

---

34 pp. 129-77, Your Children Should Know, Flora Colao & Tamar Hosansky: 1983, Bobbs-Merril Co., Indiana and New York.
35 p. 512, "The Medical Evaluation of Sexual Abuse in Children", Allen R. Dejong, Hospital and Community Psychiatry, May '85; Vol. 36, no.5.
36 p. 564, "The Justice System and Sexual Abuse of Children", Jon R. Conte, Social Service Review, Dec. 1984.

district attorney to whom the parents can direct their questions. Your rape crisis advocate will also help with this information, although usually there is not a choice about who will be assigned to defend the child.

There are two different ways to report a sexual assault. One way is anonymously by means of a third party, such as Rape Relief.[37] The report does not become part of the official police statistics, but they can use the information. The other way, direct reporting, allows the police to provide immediate protection, take a crime report and collect evidence (should parents choose to prosecute). A uniformed officer can come to the home and take the initial report. This will mean the child will be asked to talk about what happened. Then a detective will investigate the case and the evidence found: at which point a decision will be made regarding whether to accept a guilty plea or whether the case should go to trial by the District Attorney's Office.

It may be found that long periods of waiting are extremely frustrating for parents. They have the right to call the police and prosecutor to find out what is going on. They may not be able to say very much about the investigation because they also must protect the rights of the accused offender. The outcome of the case depends upon many factors which are unique to each case. Your local librarian can direct you to a listing and description of actual sex offenses in your State Penal Law Directory of Criminal Law.

Police jurisdictions vary greatly on training and procedures for handling sexual assault on children. In most districts, it is possible to back out of the

---

37   p. 20, He Told Me Not To Tell, Jennifer Fay, 1979; King County Rape Relief.

proceedings. Ideally, the system will work so that the child will be believed, the people involved will have some understanding and training in working with children and the child will not be asked to repeat what happened indiscriminately.[38]

Over the past decades, laws have been changed in favor of the victim. The offender still must be found guilty beyond any reasonable doubt, but the victim's testimony no longer needs to be corroborated. The victim is also no longer required to have resisted the perpetrator. The victim's previous conduct is no longer permitted to be used in court.[39] Two laws were passed in New York State during 1985 to assist child victim witnesses. A support person is allowed to accompany the child during the grand jury hearing as well as during the court room trial. This can be any trained professional such as rape crisis counselor, social worker, or psychologist. The second law enables a close-circuit television videotaping or screen be available for children aged eleven or younger so they need not face the offender when testifying. The statute of limitations for pressing charges is two years for a misdemeanor and five years for a felony. If the statute is up or if the family decides not to press criminal charges, the parent and child may still want to report what happened. The act of reporting itself is a powerful one. It can restore the child's sense of having some control over the situation. Parents can request an order of protection forbidding the offender from coming near the child. They may also decide to sue for damages in a civil proceeding. Civil suits only

---

38   p. 66. No More Secrets, Adams & Fay, 1981; Impact Publisher, San Luis Obispo, California.

39   p. 22, "Sexual Assaults: Facts You Should Know", Hennepin County Attorney's Office, Sexual Assault Services.

require a preponderance of evidence. If the assault occurred in a parking lot or structure, the parents may be able to sue the owner for negligence.[40] This should be discussed with an attorney. Parents may request that patrol cars cover the neighborhood. For reimbursement of medical examination expenses or other costs incurred as a result of the assault, contact should be made with the local Crime Victim Compensation Board. Any action the parents take to protect themselves and their child's rights is empowering. To continue to shroud the event in silence may further reinforce the child's feelings of guilt and self-blame for what happened.

Despite the newer laws to aide child victims, it is still difficult to prove child sexual abuse in a criminal proceeding because of:

a. The lack of eye witnesses.
b. The victim is too young (pre-verbal child or infant).
c. Competency tests may lead them to be disqualified to testify.
d. Credibility may be questioned due to the child's cognitive or verbal limitations.
e. Misconceptions that a child cannot distinguish between fact and fantasy.
f. The child may retract his/her story because of pressure by family or insensitiveness of legal process or fear of offender's reprisals if acquitted.[41]

---

40 p. 22, *Surviving Sexual Assault*, Rochel Grossman, editor: 1982; Congdon & Weed, Inc., New York.
41 p. 57, "Legal Intervention and Reforms in Child Sexual Abuse Cases", Josephine Buckley; Preventing Child Sexual Abuse, Ed. Nelson and Clark, 1986: Network Publications, Santa Cruz, California.

The family requires tremendous support throughout this process. Counseling and parent groups offered through the local Rape Crisis Center, as well as advocate assistance, should be an integral part of the family's help system at this time. The court process perpetuates and prolongs the family disequilibrium and state of crisis. Parents tend to obsess around what will happen next and energies are drained into focusing on the next court date. The child needs help to maintain a sense of normalcy despite these ongoing court activities; perhaps through hobbies and sports. The decision to seek ongoing counseling must be the child's decision so he/she can gain a sense of control over at least some decisions in their life amidst the powerlessness created by the assault and resulting litigations.[42]

Child victims not only suffered a violation of their rights, but a violation of their body. Not only are they confused, angry and bewildered by their own feelings, but they must also cope with the anger and frustration displayed by the family. Even though this may not be verbalized, it can be overwhelming for them. The child's guilt stems from feeling responsible for the disruption and upset they have caused the family after disclosure. They have a feeling of alienation and feel "different" as a result of what's happened to them, created by the reaction of others finding out and because it may have felt good even though it was a "forbidden act".[10] How the child is feeling about what happened should he addressed during the interviewing phase of reporting. It can be helpful to take the child to

---

42   p. 322, *Handbook of Clinical Intervention in Child Sexual Abuse*, Sgroi, 1982; D. C. Heath & Co., Lexington Books, Massachusetts.

an intake screening at the local Victim Counseling Center or Rape Crisis Center. The child must be helped to understand that what happened was not their fault and they are not responsible for what happened – the perpetrator is.

4. PARENTAL DILEMMAS

There is probably few more painful traumas for a parent to endure than to learn that their child has been sexually violated. It is an event that will continue to haunt and disrupt a family's life long after its occurrence. Parents experience a wide range of emotions as a result of their child's sexual assault: shock, rage, helplessness, fear and, most of all, guilt. Parents blame themselves for not protecting their children from this hideous crime. They badger themselves repeatedly with "if only I had" statements. The sad fact is, no one can be with their child at all times and protect them from every possible hurt. It is very difficult for parents to accept that it happened and that they were unable to prevent it. Parents need to turn their focus from self-blame to positive action by seeking help for themselves and their child.

A common initial reaction is shock or disbelief. Even though it may be difficult for the parents to fully comprehend how or why this happened to their child, they still must convey to the child that they believe what the child has told them. The parent must also explain that what they find hard to understand is why any adult would do something that could harm a child. A young child may not perceive what happened to them as harmful if it did not hurt. They will only perceive it as wrong if the offender told them not to tell their parents or implied a threat if they told. The parent's emotional reaction will reinforce their guilt for not telling right away and by feeling responsible for not telling them. It is normal for parents to have and express very strong reactions to finding out their child has been abused. They must try to explain to their child that they are angry at the person who tricked the child, not him/her and they are glad the child told. The child should be commended for his/her honesty and braveness in being able to tell what happened. Reassurance by the parents is also necessary for the child to let them know they want to help them feel safe and protected.

If possible, the parents need to keep their feelings and reactions separate from those of the child. The child's feeling may be completely different than the parent's. For instance, the child may he concerned that the offender is mad, whereas, the parent's concern is the child's well-being and how this has affected him/her. The child needs to be free of the parent's concern until his/her own concern is answered.[43] It's hard for parents to focus on what the child needs and deal with their own anger at the same time.[44] This is why it is so important for parents to join a support group where they can ventilate their feelings and share their experiences with other parents who are going through it also.

How effectively the parents handle the problem can greatly affect the child's healing process. Explaining to the child what steps they intend to

---

43 p. 64, *No More Secrets*, Attains & Fay: 1981, Impact Publishers, San Luis Obispo, California.
44 Ibid.

take to seek help and taking time to answer any questions the child may have is important. If parents don't know an outcome, they should say so and let the child know that they will try to find out. They can explain to the child that they are not alone and although this was an uncomfortable experience, it won't always seem so bad as it does now. Also, reassuring the child that they love them and will support them through everything they can is very helpful. Parents need to repeat that no matter what happened, it was not their child's fault. Being honest about feelings and admitting when they are sad and feel bad about what happened to their child is also important. They should present getting help in a positive light and let the child know that they are there to listen whenever he/she wants to talk about what happened. They should not constantly bring it up, but let the child approach them and set his/her own pace.

Because the offender is usually someone the child trusted or liked, angry threats made about what should happen to the offender make the child feel guilty for telling. Parents must try to place the blame and responsibility with the offender in a realistic way. Stating that what the offender did was wrong and unfair and that he/she needs help so he/she doesn't do this again to anyone else is also helpful.[45] Confrontations with the offender are better left to the authorities.

Parents must face very difficult dilemmas involving: having to restrain from expressing their own strong feelings so as not to overwhelm their child; deciding about pressing charges and the effects that a trial might have on further

---

45   Ibid.

traumatizing the child and family; agonizing over a child who won't talk at all about who and what happened, but is exhibiting definite symptoms.

Many children are embarrassed by what occurred and request their parents maintain a code of silence. To keep their child's trust, they find themselves in the uncomfortable position of evading the truth when friends, relatives or neighbors ask questions about their child. A child's symptomatic behavior or a sudden drop in academic performance may cause the school personnel to become concerned for the youngster and implicate a problem at home. The parent must decide if he/she wants knowledge of the assault to become known since it will most definitely be noted in the school records that will follow the child for years afterward. Who to tell and not tell becomes a complicated and troublesome problem for most parents to encounter. They need to sort out their own feelings so it becomes easier to convey to someone else what happened. Sometimes they tell a family member, expecting them to be supportive and they instead ask the parent how they let that happen. After working so hard to fight back the guilt, someone significant to the parent puts the blame right on their shoulders. That is a powerful blow from which to recover. Most people that do not understand the dynamics of sexual assault do have a "blame the victim" perspective. Parents may also have thought: Why didn't my child know enough to stop and run away and come to me? When people are truly powerless, they do not stop to challenge authority, they often accept society's rules and dictates blindly. How can we expect children to act otherwise?

If the offender was someone that the parents trusted and liked, the family is usually overwhelmed with a feeling of disbelief and betrayal. The child also feels more guilty for destroying the friendship by his/her disclosure. If the child was somewhere he/she was warned against, he/she may be more fearful of being punished for breaking a rule rather than for revealing the sexual assault. Not telling the whole story or changing some of the details to protect themselves usually works against them. They need to be reassured that telling the truth is more important than anything else and they will not be punished in any way for what happened.

Adolescent victims pose an even more difficult problem for parents. The assault creates for them a greater feeling of dependency on the parents whom they need to separate from as an age-appropriate life task. Their natural impulse of rebellion may be escalated by the crisis. They may carry a great deal of anger and resentment about what has happened to them and direct it to parents by constantly pushing limits, breaking rules and starting fights with family members. Unfortunately, the youngster is usually in total denial about the assault and will reject all forms of getting help even though he/she may desperately need it. Most often the anger is directed at mother who is the safest person who the youngster knows he/she can manipulate by guilt into "understanding" and tolerating his/her extreme behavior. As difficult as it may be to ignore the mood swings and not take the behavior which feels like frontal attacks personally, this is the only way to help the youngster take responsibility for him/herself and separate. As long as the parents take over responsibility for the child, the child will unknowingly perpetuate his/her feelings of helplessness, impotence and rage, which he/she will continue to direct at the parents. The parents will have to take a giant step backwards and let the youngster know that although they love them very much and they know the youngster has had to go through a terrible thing, the child's behavior is out of control. While letting the child know that the parents recognize his/her need for help and should seek it out, it should also be conveyed that he/she has no right to treat the parents poorly because of what has happened to him/her. They need to comfort the child but let him/her know when they are running away from their responsibilities by unloading on the parents, which is not fair. Parents must refuse to take over for their child, letting him/ her know that they want to help but cannot if the child is not willing to face the problem and do something to help him/herself. They need to encourage the youngster by telling him/her that they know he/she is capable and has the ability to get him/herself back together, but should seek the advice of a counselor if he/she feels immobilized right now.

    The crisis creates a complete disruption in family functioning. Often husbands and wives deal with it differently. Men might express a wish to do violence to the perpetrator and submerge the rest of their feelings, leaving the wife to cope with the aftermath of emotional turmoil that she is experiencing with the child. This leaves the wife feeling abandoned by her husband because he will not share the burden of the problem with her and act as a support. It is common to see many more mothers than fathers participate in the parent support group, because anything having to do with the children is viewed by the husband as the wife's responsibility. It does help foster the family's healing process, however, if both parents are able to support each other through the struggle to regain equilibrium.

Another common reaction is for parents to become overly protective of their children after the assault. They become very fearful that it could happen again and hope that if they take enough precaution that somehow they can prevent another occurrence. Some parents find themselves becoming suspicious of everyone, especially if the perpetrator is not known or if he was a trusted individual. This is an indication that the parent has not yet been able to put the assault in perspective. Many parents in crisis exhibit symptoms similar to that of the victim, such as sleeping and eating disturbances, uncontrolled emotional outbursts, inability to resume regular routine, general disorganization, forgetfulness and preoccupation with details of the occurrence and for the offender as well as the motives. Why did this happen to my child? It is a question parents will ask themselves over and over. They may desperately begin to scrutinize their child in search of an answer. There is no answer. All children are perfect victims. Some children have the awful misfortune of crossing the path of an offender. It could happen to any child and it does, much more often than anyone likes to think.

Regardless of good intentions, parents may find it very uncomfortable to discuss what happened with their child. Children pick up on our feelings about emotionally-charged situations and quickly get the cue that a topic is taboo. To make it easier, there are now several illustrated children's books on the market that address the issue in a nonthreatening way. (Refer to the Appendix) This might be a good beginning approach that can be used to touch upon how the child may be feeling about what happened to him/ her. Parents may want to discuss with a counselor the right words to use in talking about the abuse. Trying to focus on feelings helps the child deal with the trauma. Because the child is not talking about it anymore does not mean they have forgotten. Symptomatic behavior may re-emerge months after the occurrence. This is also an indication that the child may need professional help to achieve recovery from the assault.

How the assault has impacted siblings also needs to be addressed soon after disclosure. Everyone in the home is affected and siblings may become resentful of all the extra attention the victim is getting. It is best to resume the normal family routines as much as possible. Disruptions are unsettling to children under normal circumstances. If the victim sees it can change how his/her entire family operates, it will have a stronger impact.[46] By all means, maintaining the same show of affection for the victim is essential. The child will be very aware of the sudden withdrawal of affection and interpret it as a sign that he/she is no longer loveable since this happened. It is erroneous to think that the child will repel signs of affection because of the assault. On the contrary, he/she will need extra reassurances from the parents that he/she is still okay.

---

[46] p. 145, T1.7e *Silent Children*, Linda Tschirhardt Sanford: 1980, Garden City, New York: Anchor Press/ Doubleday.

The most difficult feelings for parents to work through are guilt and self-blame. It can be as destructive, misdirected and inaccurate as blaming the victim.[47] It almost always gets played out by the parent in the form of over-protecting the child. The child needs to be able to rebuild his/her self-esteem after the occurrence. A parent's incessant precautions for the child victim imparts the message that the child can no longer be trusted alone to make the right decision. It also implicates that the assault was somehow his/her fault and due to some unknown error in judgment that he/she brought this all on him/herself and the family. As difficult as it may be, parents must let go of the child, so he/she can grow and not be afraid to separate from his/her parent's protection. Encourage group activities and outings at first. Most child victims experience symptom relief when taken on vacation or away from the inhibitive environment that remains a constant reminder of what happened. Parents also need to get away to breathe from the experience and refresh themselves, free from the preoccupation of their child's ordeal.

Children are also adept at making the most of parental guilt by using the victim role to manipulate parents in gaining special privileges that might not otherwise he tolerated. Parents should be aware of developing this dependency situation, which will create an atmosphere of resentfulness and further perpetuate family disequilibrium. They still need to set reasonable limits and cannot make up for what has happened by bending rules and laxing limits. They would then be sharing the victim role and allowing the child to control them. To use an

---

47   p. 144 Ibid.

old cliché: Two wrongs won't make a right! Allow an average period of recovery time of about two weeks to allow for the child to get over the trauma after initial disclosure. If he/she still does not want to return to school, sleep in his/her own bed, etc., this could be an indication that a phobia is developing. He/she will need professional intervention to deal with the projected fear. When a child has nightmares, ask him/her to describe what happened to help him/her to think up another outcome in which he/she has control of the monster or boogie-man. For example, the monster got caught in a big net and dropped in a hole from which he couldn't get out.

The overwhelming feelings surrounding the crisis needs to be addressed. The Local Rape Crisis Center will have these referrals. Healing is a family process that takes time. This process can be greatly aided by intervention early in the crisis and later as well on an on-going basis. When choosing a counselor for the child and/or the family, it is important to seek a professional who is experienced in dealing with sexual assault.

Children usually try to protect their parents from upset by not speaking directly to them about the assault. This is frustrating to parents and may illicit a sense of role failure. However, the parent should keep in mind that the child may be fearful of arousing an emotional reaction from the parent that he/she cannot handle. The parent needs support to deal more effectively with all the issues as they arise with the child. The victim counselor should be asked about a support group for parents. If there isn't one in existence, one should be started. It is one of the best things that the parents can do, both for themselves and for the child. The child cannot heal if the parent does not.

5. WHAT ELSE CAN BE DONE

If the parent has made the police report, the child is in counseling, and they are attending a parent support group, they have really done everything that can be expected. The rest is up to the authorities to carry through on their job. However, parents still find themselves very powerless, having a lack of control over the slow-moving process of their child's recovery, and even slower wheels of justice. Often they feel they wish there were something more they could do to gain back control over their lives.

Taking action of any type can be an empowering experience. After encountering the local system, they are apt to find gaps in service delivery and will be able to identify ways that the system could be improved or changed, based on how the case was handled. Either individually or collectively with other parents, they may want to meet with the local legislator to make suggestions and follow through by requesting to be heard at the Human Services Committee Public Hearing. Going one step further, they may decide that a particular law needs to be changed to provide better protection for children and will want to meet with their state senator. Politicians like to meet with their constituents and parents should not be intimidated by their position. They will be surprised to find how willing and easy it is to talk to their representatives when they have a specific concern. Who knows — they may find themselves lobbying in their state capitol to back a proposed bill that they influenced to change. It may not help their child's case by the time it is passed, but they will have paved the way to help thousands of other children like their own and turned something that had been a family tragedy into something extremely positive.

On a smaller scale, they may decide that it is time to make the neighborhood safer. Many localities have organized into neighborhood watch groups in which local citizens patrol the area in shifts and call the police if they spot anything suspicious happening. Although this idea was originally started to prevent burglaries, it could also serve to alert the community of a stranger or prowler in the area. Parents must keep in mind that only 15 percent of sexual assaults are perpetrated by someone unknown to the victim. However, every preventative measure is helpful. They may also ask the town board's permission to put up posters for children everywhere regarding safety precautions, to yell "No", run away and tell someone. It is also a warning to the potential offender that he is dealing with an educated community that will not tolerate any attempts to victimize their children. Another suggestion is to contact the local library about showing films about child sexual abuses for community awareness. Libraries have access and facilities to publicize these events as well.

Preschoolers need to he taught the basics of personal safety as well. Parents can make requests to the local cable channel or to the public service network to provide children's programming on personal safety for youngsters. Suggest that your Rape Crisis Center do some TV spots to further educate the public about sexual assault. They might offer to speak about the parent's perspective. Other parents will want to hear of their experience. If they felt comfortable about revealing what happened in their life, personal testimony as part of the group process is a very healing aspect of the recovery phase. They may decide to move beyond a closed circle and engage in public testimony. This can be a very powerful experience.

Parents should also make sure that the school district includes personal safety instruction at every grade level, including its special education classes. If there are any gaps, they can work through the patent teacher association to ensure each child receives this important information. Teenagers need a discussion forum where they feel comfortable asking questions about sex and dating. Parents can find out if the junior high school has a health issues or related class where there is an atmosphere of openness for "hot" topics. The youngsters would know if there is such an opportunity provided. If not, meeting with guidance counselors and other school personnel is a way to address this need.

These are just some suggestions for breaking the silence and shroud of shame that surrounds sexual assault. They are positive forms of fighting back and tackling the heart of the problem — ignorance, silence and shame. It is moving from the role of helpless victims to strong survivors.

Being creative in doing what can be done to restore the family's self-esteem, pride and feelings of self-worth is a positive step forward. Continuing to encourage the child to strive and trying new interests and achievements helps the youngster to regain his/her own self-confidence and independence. This is the best that can be done for our children and parents. Through every trauma, we discover new strengths we never realized we possessed. The process of rebuilding stimulates new growth, insight and awareness. The parent and child will survive and become closer because of it. Of course, they must expect very difficult periods, but without losing sight of the chance for new possibilities in their parent/child relationship.

In this current age of internet accessibility and cell phone usage by teens and children of all ages, they are especially vulnerable to victimization for attention-seeking while being "cat-fished" by a perpetrator, luring them to undress or pose inappropriately. If the perpetrator is an adult, this is a crime. Parents are cautioned to instruct their children and warn them against any inappropriate requests that they may encounter even from friends they trust as the "posts" could end up on the internet. Child victims have also been "groomed" by texts from perpetrators to engage in actual encounters, with frightening outcomes. The worst case scenario being a child abduction. Keeping close watch over internet and cell phone use may not be easy given all the time during the day spent apart, so keeping open lines of communication and showing keen interest in everything your child is involved in is extremely important.

REFERENCES

Adams, Caren & Jennifer Fay, *Nobody Told Me It Was Rape*, Network Publications, Santa Cruz, CA, 1984.

Adams, Caren & Jennifer Fay, *No More Secrets*, Impact Publishers, San Luis Obispo, CA, 1981.

Adams-Tucker, Christine, "Defense Mechnisms Used By Sexually Abused Children", *Children Today*, Jan.-Feb, 1985.

Ageton, Suzanne S., *Sexual Assault Among Adolescents*, D. C. Heath & Co., 1983.

Brownmiller, Susan, *Against Our Will: Men, Women and Rape*, Simon & Schuster, New York, 1975.

Burgess, Ann Wolbert, Nicholas Cron, Lynda Lytle Holmstom, Suzanne M. Sgroi, *Sexual Assault of Children and Adolescents*, D. C. heath & Co., 1978.

Byrne. Jessica Price, Edwin V. Valdiserri, "Victims of Child-hood Sexual Abuse: A Follow-tip Study of a Non-Compliant Population", Hospital & Community Psychiatry, Vol. 33, No. 11, Nov. '82.

Child Sexual Abuse: incest, Assault and Sexual Exploitation U. S. Dept. of Health and Human Services, 1981. Colao, Flora and Tamar Hosansky, Your Children Should Know.

Conte, Jon R., "The Justice System and Sexual Abuse of Children", Social Service Review, Dec., 1984.

Conte, Jon R. and Lucy Berliner, "Sexual Abuse of Children: Implications for Practice", Social Casework, Dec. 1984.

Daugherty, Lynn B., _Why Me?_ Mother Courage Press, 1984.

Fay, Jennifer, _He Told Me Not To Tell_, King County Rape Relief, 1979.

Fay, Jennifer, _Top Secret_, King County Rape Relief, 1982.

Finkelhor, David, _Child Sexual Abuse_, The Free Press, 1984.

Finkelhor, David, _Sexually Victimized Children_, The Free Press, 1979.

Gomes-Schwartz, Beverly; Jonathan M. Horowitz, Maria Sauzier, "Severity of Emotional Distress Among Sexually Abused Preschool, School-age and Adoles-cent Children", Hospital & Community Psychiatry, May '85, Vol. 36, No. 5.

James, Beverly; Maria Nasjleti, _Treating Sexually Abused Children and Their Families_, Consulting Psychologists Press, Inc., Palo Alto, 1983.

Khan, Misbah; Mary Sexton, "Sexual Abuse of Young Children", Clinical Pediatrics, Vol. 22, No. 5.

Kroth, Jerome A., _Child Sexual Abuse_, Charles C. Thomas, Publisher; Springfield, 1979.

Moore, Dianne, "A Literature Review on Sexual Abuse Re-search", Journal of Nurse-Midwifery, Vol. 29, No. 6; Nov./Dec. 1984.

Nelson. Mary & Kay Clark, _An Educator's Guide to Preventing Child Sexual Abuse_, Network Publications. Santa Cruz, 1986.

Orr, D. P. and M. Downes, "Psychosocial Adjustment of Adolescent Sexual Abused Victims", Clinical Re-search, 29 (1) A 105 '81.

Sanford. Linda Tschirhart, "Finding a Voice: Survivor's Speak About Sexual Abuse", Harvard Educational Review, Vol. 54, No. 4. Nov. '84.

Sanford, Linda Tshirhart, *The Silent Children*, Anchor Press/Doubleday, New York, 1980.

Schleslinger, Benjamin, *An Annotated Bibliography of Child Sexual Abuse.*

Cathleen Schurr & Nancy Cager, *Sexual Assault: Confronting Rape in America*, Crosse! & Dunlap, New York, 1976.

"Sexual Assault: Facts You Should Know" Hennepin County Attorney's Office, Sexual Assault Services.

Sgroi, Suzane, *Handbook of Clinical Intervention in Child Sexual Abuse*, D. C. Heath & Co., 1982.

Shamroy, Jerilyn A., "A Perspective on Child Sexual Abuse", Social Work, March, 1980.

Shen, Jerome T. Y., "Sexual Abuse of Adolescents". Adolescent Sexuality, Vol. 71, No. 6, June, 1982.

Surviving Sexual Assault, Congdon & Weed, inc., New York, 1982, Edited by Rochel Grossman.

Sweet, Phyllis, *Something Happened To Me*, Mother Courage Press, 1981.

APPENDIX A

Suggested Reading For:

Parents

The Silent Children: A Parent's Guide to the Prevention of Child Sexual Abuse by Linda Tschirhart Sanford.

No More Secrets: Protecting Your Child From Sexual Assault by Caren Adams and Jennifer Fay.

Your Children Should Know, Flora Colao & Lamar Hosansky. Teach your children the strategies that will keep them safe from assault and crime.

He Told Me Not To Tell, King County Rape Relief, 1979. Renton, Washington.

Come Tell Me Right Away, Linda Tschirhart Sanford. A positive approach to warning children about sexual abuse.

Adolescents

Nobody Told Me it Was Rape, Caren Adams and Jennifer Fay. A parent's guide for talking with teenagers about acquaintance-rape and sexual exploitation.

Top Secret, Jennifer Fay and Billie Jo Flenchinger. Sexual Assault information for teenagers only.

Children

Something Happened to Me, Phyllis E. Sweet.

Kids Go To Court Too. What you will see and do by Jill Ruzicka.

It's Okay To Say No. A book to read together by Robin Lenett.

A Better Safe Than Sorry Book, Sol & Judith Gordon. A family guide for sexual assault prevention.

ABOUT THE AUTHOR

Although now retired, Ms. Golder's career in the field of social work has spanned over four and a half decades of service. She first obtained her A.A.S. Degree in Community Service, then a B.S. Degree in Human Services, followed by a Master's Degree in Social Work. She spent 25 years in the Family and Children Services Division of the Suffolk County Department of Social Services on Long Island, New York. During that time she received numerous service awards at the state and local level in recognition of her outstanding professional achievements in advocating for the needs of children and youthful victims of abuse and neglect.

www.ingramcontent.com/pod-product-compliance
Lightning Source LLC
LaVergne TN
LVHW041544060526
838200LV00037B/1130